Funny Jokes for Kids!

Silly Jokes that Kids and Families Will Love!

Introduction

Thanks for choosing to read our book! We've set this book up to give you all 100 jokes right up front. You can scroll through to read them all. Enjoy!

Table of Contents

Funny Jokes for Kids!

WHAT DO YOU CALL A DINOSAUR THAT IS SLEEPING?

A DINO-SNORE!

WHAT IS FAST, LOUD AND CRUNCHY?

A ROCKET CHIP!

WHY DID THE TEDDY BEAR SAY
NO TO DESSERT?

BECAUSE SHE WAS STUFFED.

WHAT HAS EARS BUT CANNOT HEAR?

A CORNFIELD.

WHAT DID THE LEFT EYE SAY TO THE RIGHT EYE?

BETWEEN US, SOMETHING SMELLS!

WHAT DO YOU GET WHEN YOU CROSS A VAMPIRE AND A SNOWMAN?

FROST BITE!

WHAT DID ONE PLATE SAY TO THE OTHER PLATE?

DINNER IS ON ME!

WHY DID THE STUDENT EAT
HIS HOMEWORK?

BECAUSE THE TEACHER TOLD
HIM IT WAS A PIECE OF CAKE!

WHEN YOU LOOK FOR
SOMETHING, WHY IS IT
ALWAYS IN THE LAST PLACE
YOU LOOK?

BECAUSE WHEN YOU FIND IT,
YOU STOP LOOKING.

WHAT IS BROWN, HAIRY AND WEARS SUNGLASSES?

A COCONUT ON VACATION.

TWO PICKLES FELL OUT OF A JAR ONTO THE FLOOR. WHAT DID ONE SAY TO THE OTHER?

DILL WITH IT.

WHAT DID THE DALMATIAN SAY AFTER LUNCH?

THAT HIT THE SPOT!

WHY DID THE KID CROSS THE PLAYGROUND?

TO GET TO THE OTHER SLIDE.

HOW DOES A VAMPIRE START A LETTER?

TOMB IT MAY CONCERN...

WHAT DO YOU CALL A DROID THAT TAKES THE LONG WAY AROUND?

R2 DETOUR.

HOW DO YOU STOP AN ASTRONAUT'S BABY FROM CRYING?

YOU ROCKET!

WHY WAS 6 AFRAID OF 7?

BECAUSE 7, 8, 9

WHAT IS A WITCH'S FAVORITE SUBJECT IN SCHOOL?

SPELLING

WHEN DOES A JOKE BECOME A "DAD" JOKE?

WHEN THE PUNCHLINE IS A PARENT.

HOW DO YOU MAKE A LEMON DROP?

JUST LET IT FALL.

WHAT DID THE LIMESTONE SAY TO THE GEOLOGIST?

DON'T TAKE ME FOR GRANITE!

WHAT DO YOU CALL A DUCK
THAT GETS ALL A'S?

A WISE QUACKER.

WHY DOES A SEAGULL FLY
OVER THE SEA?

BECAUSE IF IT FLEW OVER THE
BAY, IT WOULD BE A BAYGULL.

WHAT KIND OF WATER CANNOT FREEZE?

HOT WATER.

WHAT KIND OF TREE FITS IN YOUR HAND?

A PALM TREE!

WHY DID THE COOKIE GO TO
THE HOSPITAL?

BECAUSE HE FELT CRUMMY.

WHY WAS THE BABY
STRAWBERRY CRYING?

BECAUSE HER MOM AND DAD
WERE IN A JAM.

WHAT DID THE LITTLE CORN
SAY TO THE MAMA CORN?

WHERE IS POP CORN?

WHAT IS WORSE THAN RAINING CATS AND DOGS?

HAILING TAXIS!

HOW MUCH DOES IT COST A
PIRATE TO GET HIS EARS
PIERCED?

ABOUT A BUCK AN EAR.

HOW DO YOU TALK TO A GIANT?

USE BIG WORDS!

WHAT ANIMAL IS ALWAYS AT A BASEBALL GAME?

A BAT.

WHAT FALLS IN WINTER BUT
NEVER GETS HURT?

SNOW!

WHAT DO YOU CALL A
GHOST'S TRUE LOVE?

HIS GHOUL-FRIEND.

WHAT BUILDING IN NEW YORK
HAS THE MOST STORIES?

THE PUBLIC LIBRARY!

WHAT DID ONE VOLCANO SAY TO THE OTHER?

I LAVA YOU!

HOW DO WE KNOW THAT THE OCEAN IS FRIENDLY?

IT WAVES!

WHAT IS A TORNADO'S
FAVORITE GAME TO PLAY?

TWISTER!

HOW DOES THE MOON CUT HIS HAIR?

ECLIPSE IT.

HOW DO YOU GET A SQUIRREL
TO LIKE YOU?

ACT LIKE A NUT!

WHAT DO YOU CALL TWO
BIRDS IN LOVE?

TWEETHEARTS!

HOW DOES A SCIENTIST FRESHEN HER BREATH?

WITH EXPERI-MINTS!

HOW ARE FALSE TEETH LIKE STARS?

THEY COME OUT AT NIGHT!

HOW CAN YOU TELL A VAMPIRE
HAS A COLD?

SHE STARTS COFFIN.

WHAT'S WORSE THAN FINDING
A WORM IN YOUR APPLE?

FINDING HALF A WORM.

WHAT IS A COMPUTER'S FAVORITE SNACK?

COMPUTER CHIPS!!

WHY DON'T ELEPHANTS CHEW GUM?

THEY DO, JUST NOT IN PUBLIC.

WHAT WAS THE FIRST ANIMAL IN SPACE?

THE COW THAT JUMPED OVER THE MOON

WHAT DID THE BANANA SAY TO THE DOG?

NOTHING. BANANAS CAN'T TALK.

WHAT TIME IS IT WHEN THE
CLOCK STRIKES 13?

TIME TO GET A NEW CLOCK.

HOW DOES A CUCUMBER
BECOME A PICKLE?

IT GOES THROUGH A
JARRING EXPERIENCE.

WHAT DO YOU CALL A
BOOMERANG THAT WON'T
COME BACK?

A STICK.

WHAT DO YOU THINK OF THAT NEW DINER ON THE MOON?

FOOD WAS GOOD, BUT THERE REALLY WASN'T MUCH ATMOSPHERE.

WHY DID THE DINOSAUR CROSS THE ROAD?

BECAUSE THE CHICKEN WASN'T BORN YET.

WHY CAN'T ELSA HAVE A
BALLOON?

BECAUSE SHE WILL LET IT GO.

HOW DO YOU MAKE AN OCTOPUS LAUGH?

WITH TEN-TICKLES!

HOW DO YOU MAKE A TISSUE
DANCE?

YOU PUT A LITTLE
BOOGIE IN IT.

WHAT'S GREEN AND CAN FLY?

SUPER PICKLE!

WHAT DID THE NOSE SAY TO
THE FINGER?

QUIT PICKING ON ME!

WHAT MUSICAL INSTRUMENT IS FOUND IN THE BATHROOM?

A TUBA TOOTHPASTE.

WHY DID THE KID BRING A
LADDER TO SCHOOL?

BECAUSE SHE WANTED TO
GO TO HIGH SCHOOL.

WHAT IS A VAMPIRE'S FAVORITE FRUIT?

A BLOOD ORANGE.

WHAT DO ELVES LEARN IN SCHOOL?

THE ELF-ABET.

WHAT DO YOU CALL A DOG
MAGICIAN?

A LABRACADABRADOR.

WHERE DO PENCILS GO ON VACATION?

PENCIL-VANIA.

WHY COULDN'T THE PONY
SING A LULLABY?

SHE WAS A LITTLE HOARSE.

WHY DIDN'T THE SKELETON GO
TO THE DANCE?

HE HAD NO BODY TO
DANCE WITH.

WHAT GETS WETTER THE MORE IT DRIES?

A TOWEL.

WHAT DO YOU CALL TWO BANANAS?

SLIPPERS.

WHY DID THE BANANA GO TO
THE DOCTOR?

BECAUSE IT WASN'T
PEELING WELL.

WHAT DO YOU CALL A FAKE
NOODLE?

AN IMPASTA.

WHAT STAYS IN THE CORNER
YET CAN TRAVEL ALL OVER
THE WORLD?

A STAMP.

HOW DO YOU FIX A CRACKED PUMPKIN?

WITH A PUMPKIN PATCH.

WHAT KIND OF AWARD DID THE DENTIST RECEIVE?

A LITTLE PLAQUE.

WHAT DO YOU CALL A FUNNY MOUNTAIN?

HILL-ARIOUS.

WHY ARE GHOSTS BAD LIARS?

BECAUSE YOU CAN SEE RIGHT THROUGH THEM.

WHY DO BEES HAVE STICKY HAIR?

BECAUSE THEY USE A HONEYCOMB.

WHAT DID THE BIG FLOWER SAY TO THE LITTLE FLOWER?

HI, BUD!

WHY DIDN'T THE ORANGE WIN
THE RACE?

IT RAN OUT OF JUICE.

WHAT DINOSAUR HAD THE
BEST VOCABULARY?

THE THESAURUS.

WHAT DID ONE DNA STRAND
SAY TO THE OTHER DNA
STRAND?

DO THESE GENES MAKE
MY BUTT LOOK BIG?

WHY AREN·T DOGS GOOD DANCERS?

THEY HAVE TWO LEFT FEET.

WHY DID JOHNNY THROW THE CLOCK OUT OF THE WINDOW?

BECAUSE HE WANTED TO SEE TIME FLY.

WHAT DID ONE TOILET SAY TO THE OTHER?

YOU LOOK FLUSHED.

WHY DID THE MAN PUT HIS
MONEY IN THE FREEZER?

HE WANTED COLD HARD CASH!

HOW DO PICKLES ENJOY A DAY OUT?

THEY RELISH IT.

WHAT DO YOU CALL AN OLD SNOWMAN?

WATER.

WHAT'S A PIRATE'S FAVORITE LETTER?

ARRRRRRRRR

WHAT DO YOU GET WHEN YOU
CROSS AN ELEPHANT WITH A
FISH?

SWIMMING TRUNKS.

HOW DO YOU THROW A PARTY
IN SPACE?

YOU PLANET.

WHAT DO YOU CALL A
SLEEPING BULL?

A BULLDOZER!

WHAT'S THE DIFFERENCE
BETWEEN ROAST BEEF AND
PEA SOUP?

ANYONE CAN ROAST BEEF.

WHY DID THE CABBAGE WIN THE RACE?

BECAUSE IT WAS A-HEAD.

WHAT DOES AN EVIL HEN LAY?

DEVILED EGGS.

WHAT DO YOU GET IF YOU CROSS A PIE AND A SNAKE?

A PIE-THON.

WHERE DO ELEPHANTS PACK THEIR CLOTHES?

IN THEIR TRUNKS!

WHY DID SUPERMAN FLUSH
THE TOILET?

BECAUSE IT WAS HIS DOODY.

WHAT DID THE FLOWER SAY AFTER IT TOLD A JOKE?

I WAS JUST POLLEN YOUR LEG.

WHY ISN'T THERE A CLOCK IN
THE LIBRARY?

BECAUSE IT TOCKS TOO MUCH.

WHAT DOES A CLOUD WEAR?

THUNDERWEAR!